Glimmers of hope for those who grieve
Kelly Louise Evans

My advice;
If you can, read this at the beach.
The waves are calming,
sand is grounding,
and the sounds are healing.
Sit in the stillness,
and look for the glimmers as you make
your way through the poetry.

*Dedicated to my three brothers
Ryan, Luca and Alex*

*In loving memory of my father
Philip Mark Evans
(Big Phil)*

Authors Notes

Grief is an ocean, vast and deep, with waves that ebb and flow in rhythms that mirror our ever-changing emotions. In the throes of loss, we find ourselves cast adrift, navigating the tempestuous waters of sorrow, longing, and remembrance. Yet, within the ceaseless motion of the sea, there is a profound solace. A reminder that we are not alone in our journey.

I, a water sign, an ocean lover, see's that waves, in their endless dance, capture the essence of our grief. The rising swell of pain, the gentle lapping of memories, and the moments of calm that offer us a brief respite.

The ocean holds us in times of need, its embrace both comforting and unyielding. There are days when the waters are stormy, and we feel overwhelmed by the force of our sorrow. And there are days when the sea is calm, and we find peace in the quiet reflection of our loss.

Written by a girl whose soul needs to retreat to the ocean when feeling consumed by grief. I learnt through writing these on my healing journey, that healing is not the journey of finding joy again, it's allowing all the emotions to co-exist together so you can find balance in their presence. Letting grief, joy, pain, and love, live side by side, without silencing one to hold the other.

Through these poems, may you find a space to honour your grief and the memories of those you have lost. May the imagery of the ocean offer you solace, as it reminds us of the natural cycles of life and the enduring strength we possess to navigate through our deepest sorrows.

As you read, embrace the waves, let them carry and guide you and may you find the comfort and strength to keep moving forward.

From my soul to yours,
Kelly Louise Evans

Contents

Chapter 1 - *The Moment of Loss*
The Whispering Shore..6

Chapter 2 - *Denial and Numbness*
The Shallow Cradle.. 35

Chapter 3 - *Anger and Release*
The Vast Blue Expanse..59

Chapter 4 - *Bargaining with the Light*
The Glimmering Realm...81

Chapter 5 - *The Decent into Sadness*
The Twilight Veil..106

Chapter 6 - *Acceptance and Stillness*
The Silent Abyss..136

Chapter 7 - *Transformation and Rebirth*
The Forsaken Deep...166

The Whispering Shore

Chapter 1: The Moment of Loss

Where the ocean kisses the land and grief first touches, dancing with the rhythm of the tides, gently pulling you into a new and unfamiliar space. The echo of what once was lingers, fragile and fleeting whilst the world breathes with each wave.

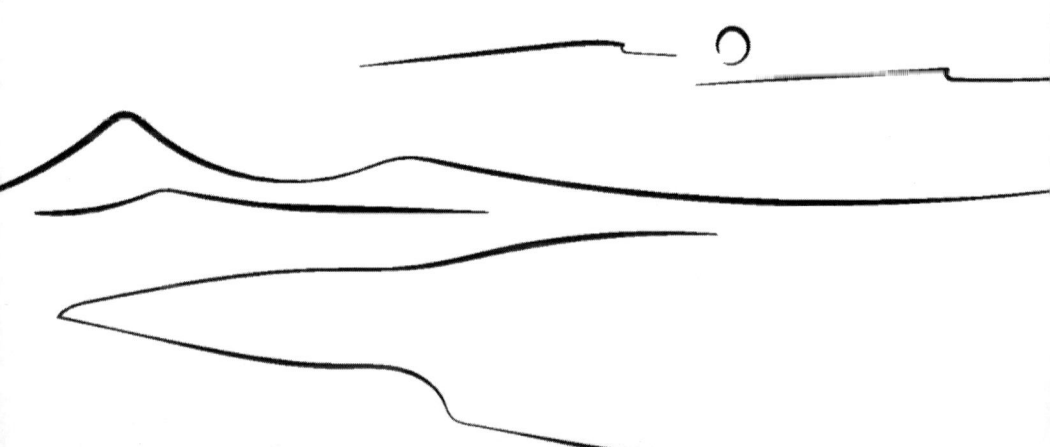

In those first few days,
I remember wanting to keep the world at bay,
as if by staying silent,
the nightmare would remain unreal.
To speak it aloud would be to give it life,
and I wasn't ready to let it breathe.
I stood by the shore,
watching the waves churn,
thinking, how can your storm pull me under,
when I've barely begun to understand its weight?
The silence too, felt like poetry,
a delicate space where knowing and denial coexisted,
where grief was a shadow,
still muted, not yet full.
I held my breath in that fragile quiet,
afraid that if I gave it a voice,
if I let the grief speak,
it would never fall silent again.

You died and yet I long to tell you how it feels,
I need to feel the warmth of your arms wrapped around me tightly,
the safety and securing that warmth and feeling gave
whilst I show you the hole that now exists in my heart,
and the emptiness that swallows my soul.
I need you to hold me whilst I scream at the world,
asking it why,
why you?
You have died,
yet you are the only one who can comfort me through it.

Grief touches gently here,
whispering at the edges,
a presence I can sense but not yet feel,
lingering just out of sight.
Life hums beyond the shore,
moving, shifting,
but I remain still,
caught in this tender pause,
as disbelief cradles me in its arms.
The current swirls beneath,
yet I do not sink,
not yet ready for the depths to take me,
for the heaviness to fill my bones.
For now, I float,
in sunlit waters,
where sorrow is a shadow,
that hasn't yet claimed its form.

The moment I found you,
I shouted at death,
like death could hear me.
As the days went on,
I asked a thousand whys.
All my questions,
doubts,
and fears,
answered with silence.
Everyone is so quick to tell me how strong I am,
and how tough you must actually be,
but no one has a choice to survive grief,
it's not optional,
nor exclusive,
it consumes your every day,
taints life a little grey,
holding those memories at bay.
It won't hesitate to remind you that everyone you love
will pass away one day,
so, say everything that you want to say,
and don't let the smaller things get in the way.
Although you may not understand what I have to say,
please don't take my soft heart and love for granted,
for I understand what is at stake,
because I have had to let someone go,
and trust me,
it's not a feeling you wish to know.

Where the ocean meets the land,
grief arrives softly,
like the first brush of a wave.
It pulls at your soul with the rhythm of the tide,
inviting you into waters unknown,
gently coaxing you into the vastness,
of what has now changed.
The echo of what was,
still lingers in the air,
like a fragile whisper carried by the wind,
fading with each breath the world takes.
You stand at the edge,
where memory and reality blur,
feeling the pulse of the earth beneath your feet,
and the vast ocean before you.
It's here, in the quiet dance between tides,
that grief tenderly holds you,
not yet overwhelming,
but present enough to know,
you've been touched by its depth,
carried into a space,
where you will never be the same,
yet somehow,
you are held
by the rhythm of its gentle pull.

The world feels unfamiliar to me now,
I feel like a stranger in this new life.
There was before,
with you,
and now after,
without you.
I feel like a guest that's visiting,
ready to go back to my normal life.
It's like I don't belong here,
like I once did.

In the first weeks after loss,
there is a hollow place inside,
where echoes of what once was,
linger like shadows in the corners of the mind.
The world feels distant,
a muted hum beneath a heavy sky,
and the days stretch long,
yet slip away like water through open hands.
Moments arrive,
familiar and strange,
yet nothing fills the space they leave behind.
The heart reaches out to the past,
only to find the empty silence of what's gone.
And still,
the world spins on,
but you are lost,
adrift in a sea,
of what will be.

A part of me went with you on that day,
the day you were taken,
unexpectedly.
I can't muster the strength to re-visit it,
it seemed to be a never-ending day,
parts hazy,
parts crystal clear.
The whole world going on around me like a normal saturday,
whilst my heart broke into countless pieces.
It was the toughest day of my life,
yet the most memorable in the most oxymoronic way.
That's grief for you,
they say.

The pain of grief is like never ending waves of broken glass,
with no time to heal between each wave,
getting wounded,
again and again.

I never experienced the feeling of homesickness,
till I was homesick for arms that could no longer hold me.

I stood on the shore,
watching the waves pull something precious away,
the sea,
vast and endless,
whispering a new kind of goodbye.
Before grief,
goodbyes were soft,
they meant "I'll see you soon,"
a gentle parting with the promise of return.
But now,
with the ocean's pull,
that word stings,
a goodbye for good,
an ache that reaches deep into the heart.
The tides no longer bring them back,
only carry them further into the depths,
out of reach,
beyond the horizon.
The waves keep rolling,
but each one carries a piece of that final farewell,
and the meaning of goodbye,
has forever changed,
like something once close,
now drifting into the vast unknown.

I have lost count of the number of times I have
watched the sun become the moon,
and the moon become the sun.
The moon has told me to rise,
and the sun said the show must go on.
The simple act of breathing leaves you exhausted,
how am I supposed to thrive in this life,
when I can barely survive.
I spend days in bed,
debilitated by loss,
realising that grief is when you hit rock bottom that
exists after the rock bottom.
You're in the in-between,
the part where you can feel their warmth,
and the next,
where they are no longer.
I attempt to cry you back,
but the waterworks are running out.

Grief isn't just carried in the heart,
it's held in every part of the body.
It's stored in the hips,
so much so that when we move to release,
it's powerful enough to quiver our lips,
and cause our chins to dip.
Our throats are burning,
and our hearts are yearning.
And although everyday our legs carry us through the day,
our shoulders carry the price we pay,
for loving someone do deeply.

People keep telling me,
that life will continue,
but to me,
that's the saddest part.

Grief is the only kind of heartbreak that will repeatedly occur.
It's like being in a war that has no ending,
for love is eternal.
So just when you thought you had put majority of the pieces back together,
emptied the water works,
learnt to be genuinely happy,
and had it all under control.
You're suddenly in the no-mans land,
the warfare continues,
and your heart shatters,
all over again.

That first time,
that first time something happens and all you need is
the person you lost,
you thought you were fine,
but this is unbearable,
heart-wrenching pain breaks your heart all over again,
you want to scream 'Where the hell are you?!'
and even though you knew,
that these moments would come,
I think I'd prefer to be numb,
than this soul crushing pain that I've succumbed.

It's midnight,
I've realised that death does not wait till you're ready,
even when you're kneeling,
begging,
and pleading to be healing,
there's nothing left to break,
this is all my heart can take.

Grief clings to me like sea creatures on the ocean floor,
anchored to my heart with unshakable force.
It has knocked me down to the depths,
where light barely reaches and the pressure is heavy,
Where pain, like barnacles, attaches itself to my soul,
unseen, yet felt in every breath.
Loneliness drifts like seaweed in the current,
wrapping around me in silent isolation,
as sorrow and heartbreak cling like limpets to the rock
of my being,
refusing to let go.
Jealousy swims through the waters,
a shadowed creature lurking just beneath the surface,
reminding me of days when grief didn't know my name,
and I didn't know its touch.
I ache for the time before these tides,
when I swam in the sunlight,
untouched by the creatures of loss that now hold fast.
But grief, once invited, remains,
a part of the sea that I now must navigate,
with its weight and its wounds,
and its creatures that cling,
and refuse to leave.

I don't know what is more soul destroying...
The fact that I keep looking for you in every crowd,
at every family gathering,
at our favourite restaurant,
or at our happy place,
or that you are never there.

If I could describe how us grievers are feeling it would be this,
that we are pretty dam strong,
but if someone close gave us a hug,
and said "I know you're not okay but I'm so proud of you for trying as hard as you are."
I think we'd probably break into a million pieces all over again.
Because if we are honest,
we are all hanging on for dear life.

Surviving grief takes a village,
that day your world comes crashing down,
people you know send enough flowers to fill a town,
you receive countless 'thinking of you's' that you don't expect,
they show up for you,
and catch you as you start drowning in the depths of grief.
Showing you nothing but love,
reminding you that this will be rough,
but that you are not alone,
and that they are always on the other end of the phone.

The one-year mark,
is a testament to the strength you never knew you had,
the courage to face each day without them,
and the vulnerability to admit how much you still grieve.
It's a time to reflect on the love that forever links you to them.
A love that endures beyond the confines of time and space.
This milestone is more than just a date,
it's a reflection of a journey through a landscape
forever altered.
It's learning to live with a heart both full of love,
and yet so heavy with loss.
We inherently know how to grieve,
but society tells us to do it faster.
The problem isn't us,
there's something wrong with a culture that forgot how
sacred grief is.

Life has been a bit of a blur since you left,
so many moments missed,
but I can promise you one thing,
your birthdays and anniversaries are still
celebrated earthbound,
as we raise a glass to the sky,
hoping you are flying high,
till we meet again.

My glow went out,
the day I lost you.
But on that day,
I noticed the sun shone a little brighter,
with its rays lighting up heaven,
as your light once lit up my life.
And now I look for the glimmers in every sunrise and sunset,
with beams of love shinning down,
to heal the broken hearts you left behind.

I hate being called mature for my age,
I didn't ask to be mature,
I didn't want to be emotionally wiser beyond my years,
ahead of all my peers.
it distanced me from my friendships,
because we didn't share the same interests,
and aspirations anymore.
It made me grieve the child I used to be,
because I was forced to grow up faster than I needed to.
My childhood flew,
all because I lost you,
and lost me too.

The first time you found me in my dreams,
I thought the nightmare had lifted,
my heart felt like it was home again,
you were in vibrant colour,
not the sepia-toned memory I've held onto for so long.
For a moment,
the weight of grief vanished,
and I shifted into a world where you were still here,
where the tides hadn't taken you from me.
But then I woke,
to the familiar heaviness in my chest,
eyes tired from holding back the tears,
a mind that battles through each day,
like waves crashing against rocks,
endlessly tested by the weight of it all.
Still, I hold on,
hoping, with each whispered prayer,
that somehow the storm will ease,
and I will feel you close again.

After loss,
we are forced to live a life we never asked for.
Finding a way to keep going,
and creating a new path forward is heartbreaking,
and can be terrifying.
But,
we do it for them,
because we know they are cheering us on from heaven.

A date with destiny,
or my first date with grief you could call it.
He arrived unannounced,
and it was certainly not brief.
I try to claw at my eyes,
if only they would stop streaming,
like a Netflix show highlighting the worst of this tragedy
hit season.
Grief holds out his hand,
and says, "don't worry my friend, it will come to an end",
this wave at least for now.
But I have a question for you,
Would you do it again?
Which part? I asked my new friend.
All of it, he gestured.
Yes, I said.
Feeling a glimmer,
it was hope arriving.
Good he replied,
Now wipe your eyes,
I will see you again,
when the pain starts to mend.

The Shallow Cradle

Chapter 2: Denial and Numbness

A gentle stretch of sunlit waters. Here, grief holds you softly at the surface as if suspended, still cradled by disbelief. The weight hasn't yet sunk in, and life moves on around you, just out of reach.

I float in a sea of sunlight,
but I don't feel its warmth.
The world moves on,
but I remain suspended in a place where time stands still.
Numbness holds me softly,
like a wave that hasn't yet broken,
a heaviness I can't quite touch,
not ready to feel the full weight of the storm.
I drift through days like a ghost,
the edges of life blurred and distant,
and though I know there is sorrow beneath,
I refuse to let it pull me under.
Denial whispers in the breeze,
a gentle lie I hold close,
as if this pause in grief,
might keep me safe from the fall.
For now, I hover between what was and what will be,
not sinking,
not rising,
just floating,
cradled by the empty calm of disbelief.

Curled on the floor,
I've become a shadow of sound,
silent wails trapped in my chest,
filling the night with weight,
but never breaking free.
The darkness is thick,
wrapping me in its numb cocoon,
where tears should fall but don't,
where grief is too heavy to release.
I lie there,
listening to the quiet,
to the muted cries that echo only inside.
While the world outside sleeps,
unaware of the storm,
raging behind the bathroom door.
In this space,
grief holds me still,
like a whisper too loud to voice,
but too silent to ignore.

Denial wears many faces,
it slips through days like silence,
a quiet refusal to let the truth settle in,
as if by not naming it,
grief might lose its shape,
might stay small,
tucked away in some hidden place.
It comes in the moments you pretend it isn't real,
when you laugh too easily,
when you tell yourself it's fine,
that life moves on, and so should you.
It's in the busy hands,
the endless doing,
the constant distraction,
filling the spaces where sorrow waits,
not ready to feel its weight.
Denial builds walls,
not made of stone,
but of fleeting thoughts and whispered lies,
that they'll walk through the door,
that tomorrow will feel the same,
that the heart can hold its ache,
without breaking.
Yet grief lingers in the cracks,
quiet, patient, knowing.
For even in denial's embrace,
it waits to be felt, to be known,
to teach you what it means
to love, to lose, and to live again.

Grief wraps around me like an animal caught in
the ocean's drifted debris,
tangled in invisible threads,
it traps and binds,
but I can't tear free,
and a part of me doesn't want to.
Grief is both the weight that pulls me down,
and the force that keeps me alive,
so I can feel the pain of your absence.
I am tethered to this prison of loss,
clinging to the threads of what once was,
because in the ache,
in the suffocating depths,
I still feel you near.
Even in this entanglement,
I refuse to escape,
for to release the pain would mean to let you go,
and I would rather drown in the sorrow,
than lose the last connection to your love.

Losing a parent as a young adult,
is like losing your mom or dad in the supermarket as a child,
except it's forever.

I stand at the shore,
where denial's waters gently lap,
the sea stretches calm,
and I stay here, at the edge,
refusing to wade into its depths.
The vastness beyond remains unseen,
but I know it's there, waiting.
Here, in the shallows,
I can pretend the storm is distant,
that the waves won't pull me under,
that I can control this sea of sorrow,
skimming its surface,
safe, untouched.
But beyond this line of comfort,
there's a place where the water changes,
a gentle stretch of sunlit calm.
The sea, once wild, becomes a cradle,
and though the depths still call below,
here, you float,
weightless, not yet sinking,
held in the quiet space,
between knowing and letting go.

When we experience grief,
we become vessels of the people we've lost.
We experience the sadness when we are forced to re-shape our future without them.
We grasp that sadness will always encircle the happiness.
Owning our sadness is courageous and a necessary step in finding our way back to ourselves,
and each other.

I drift through this quiet space,
unmoved by the world's motion,
a weightless shell, untouched,
where grief hums softly but never quite arrives.
I am here, yet not,
a presence without form,
floating in the spaces between.
Numbness wraps around me,
a veil of silence,
keeping the sharpness away,
and though I sense the depth beneath,
I refuse to look down,
refuse to see.
Denial cushions each breath,
whispers that it isn't real,
that I can stay here,
untouched and unbroken,
for just a little longer.
Time presses on,
but I stand still,
suspended between the world's turning
and the pain I'm not ready to feel.

A reminder for when the grief is indescribable,
the world needs you,
it needs your story,
it needs your lessons,
it needs your journey,
but most of all,
it needs your kindness and grace,
after trying to make you hard and fierce.
You may not need the world,
but it needs you.

When you left,
I walked into the ocean,
not to drown,
but to be held by something reluctant to let go.
To feel that oceanic feeling,
of being one with the external world as a whole.
To remind myself that some memories never leave your bones,
like salt in the sea,
they become part of you,
and you carry them,
just as much as they will carry me.

Sometimes memories sneak out of my eyes
and roll down my cheeks.

Grief feels like different parts of the ocean,
sometimes it's the deep blue parts,
that are content with being far away from the land,
then there are the waves that come crashing in without warning,
or slowly rolling in,
to remind you that it is there.
Then there is the ocean that becomes a tide pool
still and unmoving till another wave spills in,
bringing in the new,
and taking out the old.
Like us,
the ocean is in a constant state of motion,
of change,
but also like us,
it can appreciate the moments of stillness in the tide pools,
soaking in the sun,
staying stagnant for a while,
as well as letting the sun roll and dance off the bigger waves
as it ebbs closer to the shore.
I wonder if the ocean delights in each stage?
In the same way we should co-exist in our ever changing state
of emotions as we flow through life and keep turning the page.

Grief makes ordinary events,
land mines,
where emotions run high,
but in a completely different dimension,
to the family next door.
A sentence, smell or song can turn on the water works,
reminding you all over again that the empty space at
the table won't be filled.

Our bodies experience a metamorphosis when we lose
a loved one,
our home no longer feels like it sits on the solid foundations
of the earth any more.
As time goes on,
we compare our home to the homes around us,
that don't have broken windows,
or tear-stained floors.
Although your home may feel like a mess,
screaming from the basement to the top floor,
and crying in every room among those four walls.
But, it will also hold an abundance of love with nowhere to go.
So don't compare yourself to the houses among you,
for your home is unique and one of a kind,
and what's more important than what is in your heart and mind,
for your home is your everlasting abode.
So the next time you don't look after yourself,
give yourself the kind reminder that it is the first and last home
that you will ever own.
So learn to live in it,
pour it some love,
invite-only the most special guests in,
without tidying up,
for they will see you and love you more naturally on the inside.
Make it a place of love and solitude,
nourish it with good food,
and do movement that leaves you in a good mood.

As time pulls me further away from the day we lost you,
I'm slowly learning that part of this chapter of life,
is learning how to let pain be interwoven into the fabric of my life.
Grief is not meant to be fixed,
but to be felt.

Every day that goes by is an aching reminder that you're one
day further away from the last time you were with them.
Yet, every day that goes by,
you know is one day closer to being with them again.
It's a messy fine line of being grateful for the time you have here,
but the time you have here is without this person,
so how can you stay fully grateful?
You want to be with them,
but you want to be here.
You like this life,
but you like it less now they're gone.
Grief is truly exhausting.

The first year wasn't early grief,
it is complete and unfiltered shock,
simply focussed on survival.
The second year,
that is early grief,
which is incredibly difficult in a fresh and unique manner.
Everyone expects you to be 'getting over it',
but really you're starting to drown in the realisation that
your loved one is gone forever,
and so has that version of you before they passed.

Grief feels like being lost in stormy seas,
tossed and torn,
with no stars to guide you home.
The waves crash relentlessly,
against the fragile walls within,
and you feel as if you're breaking from the inside out,
a pain no words can truly hold.
Your heart once steady,
now drifts untethered,
with no map to navigate the world after their absence.
The waters are wild, uncharted,
and your internal compass remains frozen in time,
from the moment they left.
You're left with nothing but survival,
scrambling for breath as the storm rages on,
trying to stay afloat in a sea where grief pulls you under,
but somehow, somewhere,
you hold on,
even as the waves of sorrow carry you further from
what you knew as safe.

Don't let the guilt of grief eat you alive,
there's no need to feel bad,
if all you have done,
is sit on the sofa and feel sad.
If you cancelled plans with your friends,
forgot to shower,
and cried yourself to sleep.
Today was made only for survival,
and that's okay,
if that's all you managed today.
There will be better days ahead.

She doesn't know how to feel right now,
one minute she feels like she's healing,
the next she's questioning how to live at all,
one minute she's laughing and smiling,
the next she's crying whilst desperately keeping it together,
hoping one day,
it will make sense.

In the thick of grief,
what people who haven't passed over into the realm
of grief realise,
is that a part of you died that day too.
They don't look further than your surface smile,
to see how you are gasping for air.
They don't see how you flick through old photos and
videos longing for the 'old you' back.
Not only are you grieving your loved one,
you are grieving for yourself,
the person that you lost,
in the moment you found out the person you loved oh
so very much has passed.
You experience the ironic reality,
that they are no longer here,
and neither are you,
except you are still here,
wadding through the thickness of grief.

Remembering you for longer than I've known you is
completely destroying me.
So please,
share a glimmer with me everyday,
to remind me that you're there,
in some way.

In the early moments of grief,
it feels like standing at the shoreline,
where the waters stretch endlessly,
and small fish dart playfully in the shallows,
a glimmer,
a whisper of something just within reach.
They invite you closer,
their delicate movements a promise of ease,
but as you lean in,
they slip away,
vanishing into the depths.
You question: were they a tease,
or were they a gentle nudge,
asking you to lean deeper
into the ocean of your emotions,
to feel the weight of what is lost,
rather than retreat into distraction?
Each time you near,
the illusion fades,
but in their retreat,
you're drawn forward,
not away from the pain,
but into it,
a call to surrender to the waves,
and let yourself feel, fully.
For in the emptiness left behind,
you begin to see,
the first small flicker of healing is in the very act of leaning in,
allowing the discomfort to wash over,
until you learn how to move with it,
instead of away.

The Vast Blue Expanse

Chapter 3: Anger and Release

An endless horizon where the sea and grief open wide, overwhelming in its vastness. There is no escape from its reach, and anger rises like a storm across the open sea.

An endless horizon stretches before me,
where the sea and sorrow merge into one,
a boundless expanse of weight and water,
with no shore in sight,
no place to run.
Grief unfurls like waves,
wide and deep,
its reach relentless,
pulling me in.
The vastness swallows all sound and light,
and I am left to drift within.
Anger rises like a storm,
a wild wind across the open sea,
raging, howling, shaking me free.
There is no escape,
no shelter from the swell,
only the roaring tide that surges high.
The sea and grief,
the storm and sky,
all blend together,
infinite and wide.

Grief is a million things,
not just one feeling.
Sometimes grief is so loud,
you are suffocated and can't hear your own thoughts,
and other times it's so quiet,
you can hear the echos of memories and moments left behind.
Sometimes grief can be out of sight,
you won't hear from it in days or even weeks,
and at other times it screams so loud it seems to be the only company you can keep.
Sometimes grief is crying so hard you're holding your hand over your mouth to stop yourself from wailing,
and other times it's just an excuse to give your friends for bailing.
Grief is never just one thing.
but a million of them.

The truth is,
the facade of strength is a shield against
the fear of letting grief wash over you,
leaving you adrift in its wake.
Your confidence takes a hit,
and the person you were before,
seems like a distant memory.
It can feel like a never-ending struggle,
to regain your footing,
let alone your confidence.
It's a profound adjustment,
redefining your identity,
and finding new ground.

Waves of sorrow crash and recede,
in their rhythm my soul finds a need.
Each wave represents a tear that falls from my eyes,
lost in the vast expanse of the skies.
The waves,
they cleanse,
they wash away,
the heaviness that haunted my day.
Their murmurs soothe,
though the pain persists,
in their dance,
a promise exists.
Though the sea roars with a thunderous might,
there is comfort in it's endless flight.
Grief and waves,
they intertwine,
in this dance a sorrow divine.
Each wave is a heartbeat of the sea,
a reminder that grief, too, shall be,
part of the ebb,
part of the flow,
in the tides of life that we come to know.
That through the waves,
the tears,
and the gasping of breath,
we find our way,
even through death.

Grief finds me by the ocean's side,
where the waves embrace,
cradling my heavy heart,
as the tears abide.
Waves hold me,
in their gentle sway,
whispering "it's okay to feel this way".
They carry the weight of my deepest sorrow,
promising hope in each tomorrow.
The depths of my emotions,
vast and wide,
mirror the oceans endless tide.
The salt in the air,
a taste of my tears,
the ocean knows,
it's held them for years.
It understands the ache,
the silent cries,
in its vast embrace,
my spirit lies.

I feel like I'm screaming but no one can hear,
no one will ever understand how much it hurts,
even the people that are near and dear.
You feel hopeless,
ashamed that someone could be that important that without them you feel nothing.
Life will never truly be as good,
because every single milestone in life is stained with a sadness,
of your absence and what could have been.

Never underestimate the energy it takes for you
to look like you are coping with grief.
Let that mask drop darling,
you're safe to feel without masking,
rest and recharge.

Grace was always a word I associated with the olden days,
never did I think that grief would teach me such grace.
For allowing that lump in my throat,
and tears to flood my face,
as I struggle to stay afloat.
It's giving myself the grace to fall apart,
in a world that expects you to be so strong.
yet simultaneously giving myself the grace,
to enjoy the good moments,
in a world ever so dulled by your absence.
It's graciously reminiscing on all the memories,
yet holding on so tightly to everyone at goodbyes,
enough to maybe not let the universe take them away,
but graciously preparing myself,
just in case.
If there is anything grief has taught me,
it's how to live with such profound gratitude and grace.

When you're in tears and at a loss with how you're
going to live life after the loss of a loved one,
let it out,
let the emotions be felt,
seen,
and heard.
Cry as much or as little as your body is asking you to,
you will survive.
They are holding you with their love for you.
Remember, they are energy,
and you are energy.
You are connected through the energy of your love,
and I know it's not the same,
and that you'd do anything to have them here.
Ground yourself,
breathe,
they will help you find peace,
and remind you that the clouds were not made to stay,
but the sun was there to shine.

Grief sits at the table where you used to be,
sepia-toned memories flick through my mind,
making me want to flee.
But it's Christmas,
there's no where else to be.
And whilst your love keeps me company,
I feel the grief strapped to my chest,
heavy and unrelenting,
despite me trying to smile my best.
I feel the grief trapped behind my eyes,
overflowing and insistent,
putting me to the test,
yet invisible to those around me,
all merry and carefree.

One of the hardest realities of grief,
is that it hits you at any moment.
It hits you like a wave,
and you have to stay afloat,
whether you're at work,
on a dog walk,
at the gym,
or on your way to see friends.
You just have to learn to deal with it,
and ride that wave.

Healing feels like the clash of warm and cold seas,
where chaos churns and swirls beneath the surface.
There's no paycheck for this kind of work,
only the toll of grief,
not just for who I've lost,
but for the person I might have been,
had the storm not torn through my heart.
The years slip by in a haze,
like debris carried in turbulent tides,
lost to the mayhem of my mind's unrest.
The wreckage follows me, relentless,
until I finally turn to face it,
cry, release, and grieve.
It's only then,
in the eye of the storm,
that the winds quiet,
and the rewiring begins.
A slow, steady healing,
from the depths of the collision.

Death anniversaries are the most oxymoronic days of the year,
it's like reliving the worst day of your life,
yet the world keeps going by,
people go on with their normal routines,
whilst you're stuck in this moment of remembering,
trying to fathom how it has been another year without them.
You realise how much has changed since they have been gone.
You feel all the emotions,
flip through old photos,
reminiscing memories shared with them,
it's a tough day,
but it's their day,
a day to honour their memory.

You were the person who made me brave,
yet your guidance is what I crave,
your wisdom weaves it's way through my days,
our conversations make up the framework of my future,
and your love holds the tiny last fragments of my heart
remaining in place.
I will never understand why you had to go,
but know that parts of you will forever flow,
within me and through me,
guiding me back home.

Grief is the price of admission,
the cost of the human condition,
which I'll pay over and over again,
because despite the pain,
my heart doesn't need permission,
to keep loving you everyday.
So I guess that's the price we pay,
for loving eternally,
so they say.

Now we see with different eyes,
that everyone we hold close,
will disappear one day,
and that life now carries a shade of grey,
softened by the weight of what we've lost.
We understand what it is like to pray,
because we have had to let someone go,
and little do they know,
the intense feelings that come and go.
So don't take for granted the people who have tasted loss,
for we carry a deeper wisdom of love,
because we know what it costs.
So, remember the hearts that carry this weight,
for in their silence,
their wisdom's innate.
For we have learned to love, to give and to grow,
whilst knowing the depth of what it means to let go.

When the world's asleep,
I often lay awake at night,
and take a walk down memory lane,
of all the memories that I keep.
Remembering you is so easy,
I talk about you most days,
but missing you,
is a heartache that never goes away,
It's the price I pay.
The moment that you died,
my heart was torn in two,
one side filled with heartache,
the other died with you.
Sorrow entered my life,
and every heart string began to tug,
with nothing bringing it more comfort,
than a warm hearted hug.

Trauma tends to stick to your bones,
forever entangled in you,
and at the end of the day,
they are the ones that you want to phone,
but you know that can't be the way.
So if you get lost on your journey,
not being able to tell where you end,
and where the pain begins,
remember healing isn't a destination.
There is no 'getting over it',
but merely,
continuing in spite of it.
So that the pain is no longer controlling you,
and you learn to thrive,
not just survive.
Wearing your scars with pride,
a reminder of your strength and courage,
that you did not hide.

I believe some of us are born to feel deeper,
as if the very pulse of life runs through our veins,
we don't simply watch the sunset,
we sink into it,
let its colours touch the soul,
absorb its quiet power as it washes over us.
We don't crave shallow exchanges,
we seek connections that echo like endless waves,
ones that nourish our spirit,
lift us like the tide.
We breathe in peace,
for we know that it is this serenity that makes life meaningful,
for us, and for those we hold close,
both here and on the other side of the veil.
Like the ocean, we yearn for calm,
for the stillness that lets us be present,
the waves of emotion ebbing softly,
guided by the rhythm of the deep waters
that cradle our hearts and calm our nervous systems,
drawing us closer to what truly matters.

As time unfolds,
the rawness and pain of grief still remains that I seem to hold.
The seasons change around me,
and people start to flee,
forgetting that my life has been blown up into a million pieces.
The excruciating reality of your permanent absence
continues to grow,
and rather than let the pain show,
I am forced to honour the depths of my emotions,
knowing that all those pieces will never truly fit back
together again,
the way they were meant to.
But remembering that light needs the cracks,
to guide the way on the tracks,
of this life with grief in hand,
till you feel re-grounded in the sand,
hoping that one day you will meet people who understand.

It's the unexpected little moments of sadness that
catch us off-guard.
You expect the phone call to be sad,
the funeral,
the closing of the bank accounts,
and sorting of the estate.
You know all of that is going to bring heart-break.
But then, when you want to call them to ask them the
simplest of question,
or tell them about some good news,
and you realise that you can't,
but when you're feeling this way,
they are the only person that can make you feel better.
You've been hit with that double edged sword,
and nothing can make it better.

The Glimmering Realm

Chapter 4: Bargaining with the Light

Flickers of hope and attempts to negotiate with the inevitable dance in this space, where you search for a way to return to the warmth of before, reaching for anything that remains within sight.

Flickers of hope glide like waves,
gentle ripples on the endless sea.
I reach for their touch,
stretching my hands,
yearning to return to the warmth of before.
I bargain with the tide,
whisper my pleas to the open sky,
as if I could change the pull of the current,
and find a way back to shores left behind.
But the sea remains vast and untamed,
it's depths full of whispers.
Still, I reach, desperate for land,
for anything near,
anything I can hold.
In this place where grief meets water's edge,
I search for a course that brings me home,
a way to return to sunlit shores,
or learn to swim in the storm alone.

I may be crazy,
but I truly believe that if you stare at a sunrise or sunset
long enough,
and allow yourself to feel,
you can feel the warmth of the sun hugging your heart
from your loved one up in heaven.
They are right there with you,
in that glimmer moment.

The salty ocean breeze,
whispers through my hair,
the trough of the wave moves me as my thoughts
ebb and flow through my mind.
The waves make me feel safe,
held,
felt,
all this time I thought I was experiencing the waves,
turns out they love to kiss me back,
they love to move me,
to make me aware that fear is really courage,
becoming known,
and that tears are really joy,
finally coming home.

Grief casts this shadow,
fading that inner light that once guided you.
Things that once bought you joy,
now pass by unnoticed,
moments of happiness,
are ridden with guilt.
But your light never left you,
it may seem to dimmer inside of grief,
but it remains,
waiting to be lit.
Your divine spark,
always part of you,
even in the places that hurt the most.
Reclaiming and rekindling your light,
is not about moving past your grief,
but rather integrating it,
into your lifes journey.

Slowly,
you will learn to take hold of that wild spirit within you,
once again.

When I am consumed by grief,
I go to the beach.
Where I watch the waves of the ocean,
move and flow,
much like the current emotions within me,
watching the waves roll in,
brings a sense of calm,
and inner peace,
a stillness within me.
The waves remind me that I am in power,
with these currents within me,
and not in opposition to them,
but am part of,
and flowing with them.

Those good days,
the rare moments where you find yourself laughing,
you're smiling,
almost fully in the moment,
and for a split second feel normal.
Maybe in the background of the laughter you hear your loved ones favourite song,
it's a glimmer from the other side of the veil.
You're heart smiles from the inside out in that moment,
because not only are you smiling and laughing in that moment,
your loved one is there,
experiencing it with you.

How poignant is it,
to wake up knowing,
the most beautiful soul in heaven,
cheers your name the loudest.

As the years pass,
the stages of grief continue to weave themselves into your life.
Strengthening you,
with each weave made,
and each wave rode.
A constant reminder,
that the grief will never fade,
because it's the price we pay for the love we gave.

If you have been there for me in my grief,
I owe you everything I still am,
and am becoming.
Even though I may still cry,
it's less of a reflection of the lack of support,
but more of a reflection of the fact that I simply
miss my loved ones.
But I hope you know,
I've cried a little less,
knowing I have shoulders to cry on if needed.
So, if you have loved me on my strong days,
and loved me even more on my weaker days,
believe me when I say,
I don't know that I could have made it to today,
so thank you,
for loving me as you knew,
as I am today,
and as I will be tomorrow.

Our eyes are like the ocean,
when a wave of grief hits,
we can feel lost in the current,
and it's often hard to sit.
Ground yourself in the sand,
feel it's security,
and supportive hand.
Breathe,
you're okay,
as the sun sets,
be proud of yourself for getting through another day,
even if all your did was survive.
You did the best you could,
not what you should.
Tomorrow is a new day,
where you can look for glimmers in the sky,
sent from the loved ones who have had to fly.

You've become a sensitive soul,
you're weird,
in a wonderful kind of way,
you stare at the sky,
hoping for its light to guide you.
You befriended the moon,
as if you're seeing it for the very first time.
You feel a whole ocean for people,
who cannot swim for themselves,
you'd rather take bugs outside,
than see them suffer for simply being small.
You want to be quiet,
yet long to feel seen.
Tears stream down your face,
when your heart feels the pain of others fiercely.
In a world of apathy and coldness,
you fill it with empathy and warmth.

I lost my spark when I lost you,
and I'm slowly learning that,
that spark isn't coming back.
But a new one is slowly emerging,
as I push myself out of my safe bubble,
and into new experiences that I am learning I now like.
Here's to finding my new spark,
in unexpected places.

Every wave of grief is like ripping open stitches,
over and over,
until they no longer bleed.
Eventually, you start to grow around the grief,
it starts to scar over,
evidence that the loss was once a gapping open wound.
But now as a scar,
it will sometimes throb,
and not a soul will know,
but you.

If you're reading this,
you have survived the most earth-shattering grief,
with weights on your ankles,
without a life vest,
without oxygen.
You swam your way through the waves,
the rip tides,
the high tide.
You made it to the sand,
only to discover the quicksand.
But you have survived,
you will survive,
there was never a question,
like a flower in the desert,
you survived.

What a difference,
it would make,
to give yourself the same grace,
you give to the waves,
for flowing differently,
at their own pace.
You never shamed the waves,
for arriving on the ocean shore at different times.
So why would you shame yourself,
for the range of emotions you feel.
You must simply accept,
that you must travel,
at the pace you need to,
in the same way the waves do.

It's okay to struggle,
I'm sure we were all our strongest,
happiest and healthiest,
versions of ourselves before this never-ending tornado,
came crashing into our lives,
leaving us broken,
empty,
lost and in so much pain.
But,
we were once that girl our younger self would have been so proud of,
and although you won't be that version of her again,
through this messy healing process,
as you start to peel back the layers,
you will see yourself blossoming into a better version,
that has a resilience like no other,
a heart that feels so deeply,
and that wants to help others along the way.
So, no matter where you are on your journey,
although you may want life to stop around you,
it won't,
we can only look forward to what is next in store for us,
what you have experienced will redefine what 'you' looks like post-storm.
But remember lovely,
it can't rain forever.

Glimmers remind us,
they are just on the other side,
of the thin veil between us,
they are signs of hope,
sent from our loved ones.

Grief doesn't mark the end,
it's a wave that crashes,
powerful yet temporary,
and just like the ocean,
it reminds us of a love so deep,
its strength stretches beyond the horizon.
With great love,
comes great pain,
but also a force that compels us to rise again,
like the endless tides that return,
bringing hope, even in the fiercest storms.
The ocean's vastness whispers,
"Everything will be okay",
as the waves continue to break,
they teach us that we can endure,
that love doesn't end,
it transforms, just as the sea reclaims the shore.
And so, in the midst of sorrow,
we find our strength,
carried by the current of what has been,
and what will always be.

I know that your heart is heavy,
but you're so much stronger than you know,
when the nights feel unbearable,
don't give up,
and don't give in,
know you're loved.

When we lose someone close to us,
we understand that life is measured by moments.
Both big and small,
when we look back on memories with loved ones,
they become jumbled scenes of moments,
so savour all of your future moments,
because that is all there is.

The hardest part about grief,
is when you feel your heart shatter into a million pieces.
Along the way you learn that no one else can mend it,
they can only pass you the glue,
of friendship and love,
to help you put your broken pieces,
back together.

I know you did not chose to be in such profound pain,
but there is immense power in choosing how you handle the pain.
You can choose to let it spark your growth,
rather than tear you apart,
choose to find strength in healing,
rather than remaining in the fragility of grief.
Choose to see light,
when everything feels unimaginably dark and hopeless,
choose to let the pain of grief be your biggest teacher,
when it is a lesson you did not ask for.
You can choose how this experience shapes you.

One day,
between the waves of grief,
there will be a glimmer,
that only you will notice.
Something that let's us know they are near,
and from that point on,
you will live for the glimmers.

The Twilight Veil

Chapter 5: The Descent into Sadness

A realm of fading light, where shadows grow long, and the glow of unseen creatures flickers in the depths. enveloping you in its quiet hold. This is where you sink, where grief turns inward, and the world grows dim.

Griefs paradox is holding on to that loved one and feeling like you are drowning.
Letting go and feeling the guilt of being swept out to sea, but drowning regardless trying to keep it all together, whilst everything is falling apart.

Salted tears blend with the oceans flow,
in its depths,
my emotions grow.
Waves cradle me whispering soft and low,
"it's okay to let your sorrow show".
In their gentle sway,
I am not alone,
the ocean's song,
a healing tone.

I am caught in the stormy seas,
where the waves rise like walls,
pulling me deeper,
with no shore in sight,
no breath to catch.
The sky is heavy with sorrow,
and the wind howls a grief I cannot name,
But I feel it in every gust,
in every violent crash of the sea.
I descend into the storm,
each wave a new ache,
each pull a deeper plunge
Into sadness I cannot fight.
The storm swirls around me,
a wild descent into loss,
and I lose myself in the chaos,
in the endless churn of heartache.
There's no calm here,
no moment to float or breathe,
only the relentless storm,
tugging me under,
further into the depths,
of sorrow's endless sea.

Grief turns inward,
a sacred silence where the world grows dim,
Colours fade to whispers,
and the laughter that once danced,
feels like a distant melody,
a soft echo of what used to be.
I walk through this quiet chamber of sorrow,
where shadows stretch and linger,
every thought a gentle wave,
crashing softly against the heart,
a reminder of the love that remains,
even as it aches to be felt.
Time slows, and I find solace
in the stillness of this cocoon,
embracing the tender, swirling sorrow,
where healing takes root in the darkness,
and I learn to cradle the weight of loss,
letting it shape me,
not define me.
Here, in the depths of this inward journey,
I honour the light that still flickers,
a beacon in the dimness,
guiding me through the shadows,
as I navigate the uncharted waters,
finding strength in the softness of my heart.

Loss is a heartache that makes the spirit weep,
in the quiet moments,
it lingers near,
a constant whisper,
a silent tear.

Grief is a shadow,
dark and deep,
a wound that wakes me from my sleep,
it aches and throbs with every breath,
a constant reminder of love and death.
It's pain is sharp,
a piercing cry,
that makes me question and wonder why.
Yet in it's depths,
a truth unfolds,
a lesson in the sorrow it holds.
Grief is a teacher,
harsh yet wise,
in its embrace I learn to see,
the strength and depth within me.
Grief teaches patience and grace,
to navigate this hollow space.
It shows me how to find my way,
through the darkest night to the light of day.
Though its touch is cold,
its message burns,
in every heartaches,
a lesson learnt.
To cherish life,
hold it tight,
and to find my courage in the night.

If we're using war metaphors,
grief is that moment of shell-shock after the attack.
When the dust has settled,
and you're left standing in a reality that feels both
familiar and foreign at once.
A world where the person you love,
no longer exists.
Grief, you see,
isn't about fighting,
it's about survival.
It's about sifting through the rubble of your world,
trying to rebuild something from the ruins.
That's the brutal truth about grief,
it changes everything.
It doesn't brush against your life,
it floods every corner.
Grievers didn't get a chance to enter the battle,
we already lost the war,
we had no say in the fate,
and no chance to fight back.
We are left,
scouring through the wreckage left behind,
piecing life together,
bit by bit,
in a world forever changed.

Tears fall like rain in the darkest night,
each one a testament to loves bright light.
Grief flows freely,
an endless stream,
drowning in memories,
lost in a dream.
Every tear a story,
a moment lost,
a reminder of love and it's heavy cost.
Yet in each droplet,
there's a trace,
of the loved ones smile,
their warm embrace.

Grief is the echo of that moment,
when you first felt the world shift,
when you realised they were gone.
A sudden, sharp ache that settles
into the marrow of your being,
replayed in small quiet waves,
for the rest of your life.
It does not fade,
nor vanish,
instead, it lingers,
a quiet hum beneath the noise of living.
We learn to tuck it away,
to compartmentalise,
for the sake of survival,
but it waits,
patient and persistent,
until we must face it again.
Each time, it feels familiar,
an old companion,
the pain no longer an enemy,
but a reflection of the love that remains,
a bond that stretches beyond absence,
a tether to something far deeper.
Grief teaches us this:
that to have loved so deeply,
is a gift, even when it bears
the weight of an immeasurable cost.
And in those moments of pain,
we remember that the ache
is just love in another form,
carrying us,
holding us,
through every quiet storm.

There's a silence now,
where once the world sang.
A hollow ache,
like air too thin,
and I am weightless,
adrift in a space where you used to be.
The days stretch long,
yet nothing fills them,
no sound,
no light,
just the echo of a world that shattered and when you left.
I reach out,
I even scream,
but the air is cold,
holding only the shape of what's missing,
and all that remains,
is the quiet whisper of your absence,
endless,
and empty.

It feels like a storm beneath the waves,
a pull into deep waters,
The sea once calm,
now churns,
and I am lost,
caught in the undertow of something vast,
unseen but felt in every bone.
The sky is heavy with clouds that never break,
and the sun, though it tries,
cannot touch the depths where I am sinking.
Roots of old trees stretch into the earth,
searching, yet tangled,
as if they too are trying to find the light,
through layers of darkened soil.
And yet, there is movement,
even in the quiet depths,
a slow shift,
like the ocean's tide,
knowing that one day,
the waves will calm,
and the light will touch the sea again.

It's like standing on the edge of a quiet shore,
watching waves pull away,
taking pieces of the world with them.
The tide recedes,
leaving the sand cold and bare,
and the horizon stretches wide,
emptied of colour.
Beneath, the ocean swells,
a silent force pulling down,
where no light can reach.
The weight of it presses,
an unseen current dragging everything under,
slowly,
steadily.
In the forest,
branches bend under the weight of rain,
each drop a memory too heavy to hold.
The earth sighs,
soft and yielding,
bearing the burden of what was.
Yet, somewhere far below the waves,
life stirs in the quiet dark,
waiting for the storm to pass,
for the sun to find its way back to the surface again.

Once the waterworks start,
it's hard to put an end to this healing friend.
A cathartic experience,
a cleansing of the fears,
to help the mind mend,
as each tear takes with it a heavy toll,
emotions flow freely,
a purging of the mind,
unconfined.
Behind every tear is a story,
a journey of pain and perserverance.
Allow them to be a reminder of your strength,
and a tribute to your resilience.
For once the waterworks start,
it's hard to put an end to this form of art.
a release of pain,
a surge of sorrow,
so as I cry today,
and maybe tomorrow,
allow me to wash away the troubles and thoughts,
a baptism of sorts.

Your heart breaks a little more,
when your crying at night without making a noise,
losing your breath with those silent screams of hurt.

If I can promise you one thing,
you don't know a real crying session,
until you have grieved.

"you look tired"
I'm tired of trying to thrive,
when all my energy is being used up,
merely trying to survive.

We were too young to meet grief,
why did the stars need you,
more than we did?
We were just children.

Losing someone you love,
leaves you staring blankly at the reflection in the mirror,
not recognising yourself anymore,
smile lines replaced with the shadow of grief,
eyes dull,
that have lost their sparkle,
a face that used to be vibrant and full of life,
now lifeless,
I'm just a shell of a person now,
moving through the emotions of life.

I wonder if you knew,
that the night before you passed,
would be your last sunset.

Cry little one,
let it all out,
it's nearly impossible to cry quietly when grieving someone who took up so much of your heart.
Let your hands shake as you try to wipe the never-ending tears stream down your face,
let the irregularities of your breath take over,
let your heart scream with pain,
whilst your mind races like a train through all the precious moments shared,
and those moments where that loved one's absence echoes.
Let it all out.

One thing you learn about grief is the fear that comes with it, the fear of not knowing how you will do life without your loved one,
of wondering if are you ever going to be ok again.
Trying to believe that tragedy is not hiding round every corner, that every phone call will be to deliver or receive bad news.
Of trusting happiness,
of saying goodbye to loved ones and wondering if it will be the last time you see them.
Grief leaves you riddled with fear,
because how can you now trust a universe that took someone you loved away from you too soon?

Our hearts know heartbreak,
deeper than any boy or girl has ever caused.
Our mind knows how to form and appreciate
connections that we still have on this earth,
so that it savours all the moments for us,
big or small.
Our souls know an emptiness,
that feels like it will never be filled again.
We feel grief in every limb and heartbeat,
yet it cannot be cut off or taken out.
It is there to be felt,
to remind us,
that we loved fiercely.

Grief follows you everywhere you go,
it stains your perspective of the world,
and taints your future memories.
It stops you in moments of laughter as the pain re-bubbles
to the surface,
catching you in a glare,
you feel the pain waiting to seep through the cracks and
scream whilst everyone else is still laughing.
it's a constant reminder that you have experienced
this infallible pain,
that others around the table will not be able to comprehend.
it makes you stronger when you did not want to
hold such strength,
and more mature,
when you did not ask to be wiser beyond your years.
It's something you learn to grow with,
as it's always there in the background.
So don't let it weigh you down or ignore it,
ebb and flow with it,
feel it fiercely,
knowing it does not define you or your future,
but is merely a part of you that will forever need nurturing,
just as you do too.

It's the evening before my birthday,
the day you used to greet me the loudest,
never missed,
always the proudest.
So here's to another year without your wishes,
hugs,
and kisses.
Another year of friends trying their hardest to make it special,
but no matter what the day brings,
your absence echos the loudest.

Putting the pieces of a broken heart back together feels like
putting together a jigsaw with missing pieces,
shards so tiny not even the naked eye can see,
but our hearts plea,
to find ways to be strong,
and re-build the armour,
because even though the pieces will never fit back together,
and the cracks will always show,
it's a kind reminder that light needs the cracks to be able
to shine through.
Slowly re-building our strength and courage,
to open our hearts back up to the love we deserve to receive.

Some days I'm treading water,
the next a tsunami of grief hits me.
On bad days,
I feel like I am drowning,
on better days,
I make it to the surface.
Healing looks different every day,
just like the waves in the ocean,
that rise and lower,
as they ebb and flow their destined path.

I often wonder if that longing to want to be held ever wonders.
Those quick embraces remind you that you only want
to be hugged longer.
A huge part of grief is having your security and safety swept
from under your feet.
So most days we don't just want a quick hug from a meet,
we yearn for the kind of hug that encompasses us,
making us feel like,
just maybe,
everything will be ok again.
But most importantly,
the kind of hug that has the potential to bring us that safety
and heal the irreparable pain,
because the toughest part is masking the pain from a society
that expects us to heal a lot quicker than what is doable.
The real agony comes from the expectations to be healed,
whilst still on the ground,
wounds fresh and still bleeding.
It's like they can't see our tear-stained eyes pleading,
for a real hug that makes you feel warm,
after being left out in the cold for too long.

Grief has the ability to choke you,
to make you feel like you are drowning,
after you may have resurfaced.
it riddles you with anxiety,
leaving you incapable of the most simplest of tasks.
You're so numb you don't even notice the tears streaming
down your face.
The loss of appetite,
yet feeling sick at the same time,
all whilst being consumed by the heaviness on your chest,
a feeling all too familiar.
You've returned to the safety of a feeling that has become
normal to those who have people on the other side of the veil,
but completely unknown to the rest.

Somewhere between then and now,
your face turned into photographs,
your voice turned into videos,
your favourite songs turned into reminders,
and your favourite places turned into memories.
How did we get here?
Somewhere between then and now.

The Silent Abyss

Chapter 6: Acceptance in Stillness

In this space of profound quiet, acceptance begins to take form. The world has shifted, and though the silence is heavy, you learn to carry it, to breathe in the depths.

I go to the water when I need to be held,
mother nature holds me in her loving embrace,
with each ripple of the waves,
the loneliness fades,
as I feel the wrap of her love around me.
Her love is constant and unconditional,
a soft reminder of how the love for myself should be,
when I feel too weak to hold myself up,
I let mother nature support my heavy heart,
knowing that I am never too much for her to hold.

It's okay to feel weak,
after being strong for so long,
but remember,
just like a wave in the ocean,
it rises and falls,
as will you.

Strength is knowing that you don't have to withstand the force of the waves,
instead,
you welcome the crashing waves,
as you swim in their swell,
you flow with the tide,
releasing any attempt to control the current,
and instead let it take you on it's course,
because your strength is more than just surviving the hardest moments,
it's going with the flow,
but crashing when you need to.
It's being beautiful on the surface,
but having depths far below that only you would know you've overcome,
and it's being soft,
yet unstoppable.

Years stretch on like a river of time,
marking the absence,
and reminding me of the mountain I climb.
Grief is a journey,
a road that's unkind,
with memories of the past always on my mind.
Missed birthdays,
missed laughter,
missed moments to cheer,
a void that grows wider with each passing year.
Holidays hollow,
traditions now pale,
the absence of love,
my heart's tale.
Yet in the silence,
whispers remain,
of moments shared,
amidst the pain.

Grief grips tightly,
shadows cast,
memories fade,
slipping fast.
Once so vivid,
now a blur,
faces soften,
voices fade,
and laughter echoes,
distant and faint,
scenes once clear,
now ghost like and quaint.
Clutching at strands of time,
trying to hold on to whats no longer mine.
In the silence the tears flow,
for the love that I once did know.
Yet in the fading,
the love never strains,
a whisper through the deepest pains,
and in my heart,
you still remain.

Grief is a whisper,
soft and frail,
a tender ache,
a silent wail.
Heart strings frayed,
emotions thin,
griefs touch felt deeper within.
A glass heart so easily shattered,
by memories of what once mattered.
Every word,
is a fragile sound,
yet in the silence,
pain is found.
Grief is a feather light and heavy,
a burden carried,
oh so steady.
Fragile moments,
brittle and brief,
in the quiet there lies the grief.
In it's embrace we come to know,
that strength is found in being weak,
in letting sorrow freely speak.
In fragility,
a power blooms,
a gentle light in the darkest of rooms.
Yet in this dance of pain and grace,
we find in our hearts,
a softer place.

In those moments of darkness,
it is so easy to forget your worth,
please don't let grief change the way the
world see's you,
and loves you.
Nor should it change the way you see,
and love yourself.
Handle yourself with care,
be compassionate with yourself,
the world is feeling understandably heavy,
so be patient with your healing,
and come home to yourself,
when you are ready.

There's no race to the finish line of a feeling.
You just get to feel,
until the feelings through.
Without feeling,
there is no healing.
But how do you expect to feel the emotions of losing a
person that once walked out that door and never returned.
When actually, all you want to do is to forget,
but when you are grieving,
forgetting is the last thing you want to experience.
So you are left stuck,
in the in-between,
of what you knew,
and what could have been.
Reminding yourself that those memories can always be
found behind your closed eyes,
and that the gap between us,
is only as far as it takes to feel their warmth in your mind.
So like a dense forest that you can't escape,
or big stormy seas that consume and take,
although these feelings feel that they may break what it inside,
remember to look beyond your eyes,
because even with waves that are 30-feet high,
all you can do is try.

Have you ever sat with your grandparents and gone through their photo albums,
whilst they talk about the different seasons of their life,
but get choked up reminiscing all the people who used to be.
Since losing you,
I now understand that feeling,
because as I flick through albums,
of pictures of the girl that was once me,
but isn't anymore,
I've realised that I'm mourning myself,
because death doesn't ever take one victim at a time,
the part of me that naively viewed the world through innocent eyes,
and wore her heart on her sleeve so easily,
is now crying over the gravestone of memories that used to belong to a family that was once mine.

I hope death is like being carried to your bedroom
when you're a child,
I hope you feel that warmth from your loved ones,
and know what it's like to be held,
in the safety and security,
in the arms of those,
you left behind.

See your fear,
as the newborn turtles see the ocean's pull,
uncertain, yet ready.
Sit with it, as they pause on the sand's edge,
feeling the rush of waves beneath their tiny feet.
Surrender to it,
as they surrender to the depths,
knowing instinctively that the tide will carry them.
Let every emotion wash over you,
like the saltwater guiding them,
nudging them forward into the unknown.
Feel the sensations rise within,
as they do when the ocean first embraces them,
lifting them into something vast yet nurturing.
For in this surrender,
in trusting the pull of what lies beneath,
you find the currents that guide you,
leading you to your truest self,
not in resisting,
but in letting go.

The fragility of grief is like the delicate tendrils of
seagrass swaying beneath the waves,
bending but never breaking,
held by unseen roots in the ocean's floor.
Though it appears fragile,
it moves with resilience,
surviving the storms and the surges,
anchored in a quiet strength the surface cannot see.
Grief, too, must remind you of this hidden power,
the strength that rises not in loud defiance,
but in the silent persistence,
the way you move through each day,
piecing together fragments of a heart shattered by loss.
Nothing truly fragile can withstand such a storm.
But like coral that rebuilds after the sea's
most violent tempests,
you too are anything but fragile.
For who else but the grieving can gather themselves,
time, and time again,
reforming in ways no one else can understand,
with a strength that only loss could unveil?

Grief dances in the shadows of our every day moments.
Yesterday,
laughter echoed as I reminisced,
and today,
it's replaced by a silent ache that lingers in
my heart like a heavy mist.
Tomorrow,
I may find myself smiling at your picture,
yet, the day after,
tears may stream as I journal a scripture.
It's a paradoxical journey that has to be taken at our own pace,
where smiles and tears,
show on our face,
a testament to the complexity of love and loss,
where sadness and joy co-exist,
as it seems like you're falling into an abyss.

Learning to try and control my grief was my first mistake,
we can't control when it arises,
nor does it have a routine like the sun and the moon,
all we can do is learn to ride the waves until the tide changes,
to befriend the rough, stormy waves,
knowing that they too shall pass,
but allowing their simplicity to become your greatest ally
when you feel your most alone,
letting them hold you in your vulnerability,
until you feel whole again.

Maybe as we cry about how awful the end was,
they are whispering to us through the ocean breeze,
"How I lived was beautiful. Hold on to that".
For while the waves crash with the memory of their absence,
the shimmering surface reflects a life well-lived,
each ripple a reminder that even in their departure,
the beauty of their existence remains,
etched in the rhythm of the sea,
in the pull of the tide,
in every gust of wind that touches our skin.

Grief teaches us the quiet luxury of simplicity,
like the tides that ebb and flow without notice,
the slow, gentle mornings where the world feels still,
and your body whispers its needs,
much like the ocean's call to rest in its embrace.
It reminds us that the real riches lie
in uninterrupted moments with those we love,
in the unsaid words, finally spoken,
the homemade meals that warm the soul,
and the stillness of the mind cradled in silence.
Like waves meeting the shore,
grief shows us the beauty of nourishing what's within.
As we surrender to the rhythm of nature,
watching the sunrise and sunset,
grief invites us to strip away the noise,
leaving only what matters,
just as the ocean leaves behind only its finest treasures,
after the storm has passed.

Grief is a metamorphosis,
a journey we must walk through,
when you're caught in the thick of despair,
like the butterfly grounded,
wings not yet aware.
You can't force the tears to dry,
as you look up to the aching sky,
knowing the pain will pry,
deep within places untouched,
raw and shy.
But in time, it will soften its sting,
and you'll start to feel the gentle lift of your wings.
Only then, in the quiet embrace,
will your heart make space,
to rise with the winds,
and find your place.

A gentle reminder,
you are not broken,
nor fragile,
nor in need of fixing.
What you need is a hug that holds the weight of your heart,
a space where your emotions are cradled,
free to fall apart.
You need someone to see you,
as you truly are,
without the mask you've carried so far.
Be patient with the person you're becoming,
honour the slowing down,
the whispers from your soul that long for rest,
for gentleness to soothe your chest.
You need to come home to yourself,
to the version that's faced the world's harshest winds.
Let yourself be,
not the reflection of others' expectations,
but the person your inner child yearns to see.
You are whole in this moment,
with the strength to return to who you wish to be,
so come home to yourself,
and find peace in just being free.

Only those who have walked the path of grief will understand
when I say,
once you cross into its realm, there is no return,
it's irreversible.
Your life is tainted forever,
you have felt pain unlike no other.
But in this realm, where the lessons are hard and
the nights feel ever so long,
you're not as alone as you think.
I can promise you that, sadly,
many others are riding this wave of grief too.
So, promise me one thing,
as every wave comes and goes,
watch yourself rise from the depths,
stronger,
and more together,
than you were before.

Feel all the feels,
it means you loved with your whole heart.

One day,
when you least expect it,
you will notice yourself feeling lighter,
you will dance when you make your coffee in the morning again,
you will sing in the shower,
and you will really belly laugh with your friends.
That doesn't mean that you have healed or forgotten the grief,
it just means that you are riding high on that wave,
enjoy it,
flow with it,
you worked hard for a moment like this.

I am learning,
so very slowly,
to live around the loss of you.
Comprehending that the grief doesn't get smaller,
but that I grow around it.

Let grief be your guide,
not your guard.
In the dance with grief,
we often lead with resistance,
holding it at bay,
masking our true feelings with a brave face,
because people often don't know what to say.
But what if we shifted in our steps,
and embraced the rhythm of our sorrow,
allowed it the space to merely exist,
to breathe,
to teach us?
Because as grievers if we have learnt anything,
grief isn't a sign of weakness,
nor is it a shadow to outrun.
It's a force with no shame,
to pop up and remind us of the pain.
Grief is a testament to love,
a journey through memories,
a teacher of profound truths.
So let's redefine strength,
not as the absence of grief,
but as the courage to face it,
to give it a voice,
to let it walk beside you,
so that you don't diminish it,
but honour it.
Because in that journey of honouring it,
you find healing along the way,
a deeper connection with yourself,
and a reminder that this is the price we pay,
for losing the ones we love,
but it can also be your reminder,
of the love that endures beyond loss.

We'll be okay,
we will.
There's so much light waiting to find us,
even through the darkest nights.
Grief, like the tides,
will rise and fall,
but over time,
it will soften,
and you'll find more space to breathe as it ebbs.
Each wave may still catch you by surprise,
but you'll learn what you need to survive its pull.
Just remember,
breathe your way back,
find your way home,
back to the heart of who you are,
and let each breath carry you toward the sunshine
that still remains,
waiting to warm your soul again.

Most of my life I had only heard about you through others,
you were a whisper,
but nothing more.
Till one day you consumed my whole being.
The anxiety that came with it,
amplified my darkest days,
and yet, you grief,
dimmed my brightest.
There's now doubt,
when their previously was none,
and a tainted sadness,
like a heavy dew,
over everything I once knew.
You make me feel like I am playing catch up,
in a world that won't wait.
Despite me trying to evade your presence,
I have no control over when you'll show up.
You are an emotion born out of my past,
but currently the biggest impact on my future,
I've learnt you're not just a stepping stone in the river of life,
so I think it's about time we held hands,
we let go of the pain together,
knowing our loved ones will be with us forever,
we won't move through it,
but grow around it,
living in each others abode,
unopposed.

While I only see you in the space between the clouds,
your love still blankets the earth,
like Autumn leaves when they fall.
As the seasons change,
new opportunities arise for me to turn the page,
but I always stall.
I'm constantly pulled between love and loss,
grief and gratitude,
pain and purpose.
But how brave is it to allow yourself the space to see that
seemingly opposite things can all be true at once,
to hold them all in your hand at once,
and to feel them all in your heart at once.

You are not just your grief,
you are so much more,
because of your grief.

When you feel your heart shatter into a million pieces,
remember, just as the sun sends its rays to touch the ocean floor,
light finds its way through every crack.
Even in the deepest parts of the sea,
where darkness sways,
the sun still reaches,
and through our wounds,
through every broken fragment,
its warmth flows in,
guiding us back to wholeness.
The cracks are not the end,
but pathways for healing,
for the light to seep through,
reminding us that even in the depths,
there's a place for the sun to shine again.

When the waves come crashing in,
and you feel too debilitated to keep holding your
breath underwater,
remind yourself that the waves come and go,
just like your emotions,
ebb and flow,
you always have the strength to hold on to your
breath a little longer,
until this wave passes.
You will catch your breath,
and keep going,
for you,
for them.

The Forsaken Deep

Chapter 7: Transformation and Rebirth

The deepest place, where grief transforms into something new. The unknown stretches before you, but within this forsaken space, there is the possibility of hope and renewal, as life stirs even in the darkest corners.

As a child,
I built a house in my head,
it was my father,
he was the four walls of my home,
he was the shade,
the safety,
the security,
the comfort,
and when you left,
you took 'home' with you.
So, I have had to learn to 'find' home myself.
And in doing so,
I have learnt that it is my body,
and although there are some tear-stained floors,
and pain behind many of it's doors,
there wisdom that you taught me on the bookshelves,
next to the determination,
resilience and trust,
that have had no time to collect dust.
And although at the moment ocean eyes are a must,
my heart is overflowing with leftover love.
It's beginning to leak through all the cracks in the walls,
it's spilling onto strangers and friends who sit in the halls,
telling me how I should paint my walls.
The world is filling up,
with all the love that was meant for you,
and although it's sad,
it's kind of beautiful too.

In the depths where the light barely reaches,
my soul dives deep and the ocean teaches,
that in the darkness,
there's space to heal,
and in the stillness,
the truth I feel.
The waves hold me tender and strong,
in their embrace I find where I belong.
They rock me gently,
with a soothing grace,
in their arms,
I find a sacred place.

Grief and the ocean,
they intertwine,
in their depths I find whats mine.
A place to weep,
a place to mend.
In the waves my sorrows blend,
held in their constant motion,
I find peace in the oceans devotion.
For simply letting me be,
as it holds and sets me free.

I wish more than anything,
that you could see yourself the way
your loved on see's you in heaven.

I think it's brave.
Brave that you get up in the morning,
when all you want to do is go back to sleep,
and wish for this nightmare to be over.
Brave that you continue to love and open your soul,
despite yours being shattered into a million pieces.
Brave that you choose every single day to move forward,
to keep building your self-scaffolding,
and putting one foot in front of the other.
Never forget how brave you have been,
and how brave you continue to be.

The strongest hearts,
have experienced the most profound pain,
remaining soft,
when grief tries to make you hard,
is one of the greatest accomplishments you
can make in this journey.

Let grief be one of your biggest teaches in life.
Grief makes you want to say 'I love you' at the end of
every phone call,
just incase.
It makes you want to spend as much time with your loved ones,
because we know the pain of losing someone we love.
It teaches us to appreciate the moments in life,
for when we lose someone that is all we have left.
It creates an inner strength in us,
one we didn't know was possible,
and to be grateful in ways that were different to before.
So, although grief has destroyed me,
it has taught me so much more.

I truly believe,
that the space between the sun peeping up at sunrise,
and setting at sunset,
is the space between heaven and earth.
And that's why I romanticise about it,
so that I can be a part of both worlds,
even if it is for a brief period.
To catch the glimmers,
to share a moment with you,
and to embrace the warmth,
of the hug that you send down from heaven to me.

Just like the moon,
as grievers we are both constant,
yet ever-changing,
it's okay if you have outgrown familiar places,
faces,
and spaces,
if you no longer feel connected to people who you
thought would be in your life forever,
to realise you have grown apart,
rather than together.
If everything around you looks the same,
but feels ever so different.
Just like the moon,
each phase is necessary and beautiful.
So as you ebb and flow,
and learn how to grow,
know that it is okay if you have changed.

You can do,
hard things.

Healing comes in waves,
and maybe today the wave hits the rocks,
or maybe it is soaring at it's highest vibration.
It's okay to experience either,
healing isn't a destination,
it's a beautiful metamorphis.
So, may you shed that armour that you have placed
around your heart so tightly,
and with every breath,
feel yourself evolving.
Just like the moon,
each day you will look a little different,
but you will also feel that immense power,
to bring yourself back home,
in the same way the moon brings in the tide.

The sun to me,
is the glorious lamp of heaven,
reminding me that my loved one is not so far.
The moon to me,
is my friend,
reminding me of my strength,
through these ever-changing waves of grief.
And the ocean to me,
is a metaphor of my emotions,
reminding me that the storm will pass,
and calmness will follow.

I'm grieving,
the version of me that once felt whole,
the part that helped me through the darkness,
but now seems too small to carry the weight of who I've become.
She was my anchor,
my shelter from the storms,
but now, she no longer fits,
like a worn-out coat I've outgrown.
I'm shedding those layers,
letting her slip away gently,
for it's time to step into the light,
to embrace the new rhythm that my soul is calling me toward.
It's hard, to leave behind the familiar,
the place where my heart once called home,
but I feel the pull of something greater,
an uncharted path that beckons me to grow.
Though it aches to say goodbye,
a piece of her will always linger,
woven into the very fabric of who I am,
as I carry her memory forward.
But I must grieve,
release her with love,
to honour the journey ahead,
and bloom into the next version of myself.

To the person missing someone in heaven,
it will get better,
I promise.
You will learn to oscillate between grief and joy,
like jumping in and out of a puddle.
You will form the ability to recognise a wave of grief
and be able to manage it,
till that wave reseeds.
Life will hold peace and meaning again.
You won't ever get over losing someone who took up
so much space in your heart,
but you will find a new 'normal' of living.
You will laugh again without masking,
you will breathe again without being interrupted by the pain.
You won't be able to put back every piece of you
that grief broke,
but with the right self-scaffolding,
you will heal enough of the pieces,
that you start to see the glimmers.
So one tear,
one breath,
and one day at a time,
you will make it.

One day,
you will tell people how you pulled yourself out of the ocean,
when you couldn't even swim.

Waves feel different when we ride with them,
when we surrender to moving with them,
time slows.
We paddle into the energy that scares us,
but instead of letting it consume us,
we try desperately to become one with it.
We catch a new perspective,
we ebb and flow with the wave,
with our fear swimming around us.
Rolling in with the tide,
we give over to it,
much like when we experience the crashing waves of grief,
we must allow ourselves to flow with it,
knowing that the crash will eventually feel
like a soft crash landing.

Don't get me wrong,
grief is the most earth-shattering pain,
anyone can feel.
But through all that sadness and sorrow,
the universe gives us reminders,
of how beautiful endings can be.
When the sunsets,
and the moon rises,
it gives us opportunities to heal,
through the glimmers sent from our guardian angels.
To allow the tears,
feel the fears,
and to watch them stay with us over the years.

Grief is being in a city at night filled with lights,
yet one by one,
the lights start to go off.
The City is a metaphor for your heart,
and the lights are the broken pieces of your heart
slowly losing their spark.
You're learning to live in the dark,
it's becoming normal.
Your heart is closed off,
and life is passing you by.
But what if, ever so slowly,
you started to open your heart back up.
You saw that the 'good' people in your life are
trying to help you turn those lights back on,
and guide you back home.
Those lights slowly turning back on are the tiny
fragments of your heart,
glueing themselves back together again.
Now, these lights can't turn on all at once,
but with strength and courage,
love and support,
I think it's worth seeing how many lights you can turn back on.

Grief is a portal,
a doorway into a new reality.
But what if, just for a moment,
we changed how we looked at it?
Those feelings we fear,
the ones we pack away,
are some of the truest emotions,
we will ever know.
They are not the enemy,
but a springboard into a new life,
where you feel more deeply,
where the world becomes clearer,
as if seen through a new lens.
Grief cracks open the heart,
making you aware of the body's wisdom,
of the nervous system's quiet language,
a language most never learn.
And when you come to peace with it,
when you stop resisting the pain,
grief becomes a guide,
Taking you to the highest version of yourself,
soft-hearted, yet stronger for what you've faced.
In that softness lies a quiet power,
a resilience born not of hardening,
but of allowing all that is real,
to flow through you,
and shape you with grace.

The loss of tragedy is too vast for the mind to comprehend.
Even the wisest thoughts fall short,
unable to soothe a heart that bleeds.
In moments like these,
you must go deeper than the mind,
to love, to have faith, hope, and purpose.
It is the body's wisdom you must lean into,
the knowing that lives within the bones,
where true healing begins.
For our bodies do not just crave healing,
they long for connection.
Whether it's the gentle ebb of the waves,
the warmth of sunlight on your skin,
or the soft touch of a dear friend,
these moments of connection are more than comfort,
they are the organic rhythm,
that helps regulate a heart shattered by tragedy.
In the quiet of connection,
the heart begins to mend,
the mind begins to soften,
and slowly, piece by piece,
we are reminded,
that even in the darkest loss,
we can find our way back,
through the wisdom of the body,
and the power of connection.

You still feel like home,
after everything we've been through,
after all this time,
you still feel like home.
Your warmth,
safety and fatherly advice.
I try to deny it,
showing myself the home I have made,
with walls I've raised,
and people I've found,
but it's not the same,
no shelter can compare.
I can't try and hide it,
you were, and always will be, my home.
I wish you'd come back,
because I ache for the comfort I knew,
to be held by the arms that had been home for 25 years.

The pain in the heart of a griever is heavy,
a weight too deep to measure,
yet it teaches me something more,
not to let it harden,
not to close the door.
Instead, I keep the heart soft,
letting the ache flow through,
feeling it fully,
but not allowing the wave to pull me under.
Simply acknowledging it,
as it whispers its truth.
I listen to the pain,
letting it be heard,
letting it move through my body like a river.
For in feeling it, but not becoming it,
I learn that emotions are not my enemy,
they are messengers,
guides,
each one with something to teach.
The heart stays soft,
not as weakness, but as strength,
and in the depths of pain,
I find the wisdom to remain whole,
to feel without breaking,
to grow without closing.

In the darkest days of grief,
there is a breaking open,
a shattering of all that once seemed whole,
and from that space,
a transformation begins,
slow and unseen.
Your values shift,
roots grow deeper in the soil of what truly matters,
and your outlook on life softens,
expanding to embrace the fragility,
the preciousness of every breath.
It's here, in this darkness,
that you learn to live differently,
to see the strength in surrender,
and to understand that emotions are not enemies to conquer,
but waves to ride,
each one shaping you,
into something new.

To anyone who has lost someone they loved,
I am sorry that this infallible pain is all too familiar to you.
I am sorry that we are in this realm together,
where the world has dimmed,
and time goes faster,
yet also slower than it ever has before.
Where everything feels exhausting,
yet some days you're able to escape the pain,
and see that joy can co-exist with grief.
But then other days you're jolted back into survival mode,
and you go through the days in slow motion,
doing whatever you can,
to get to the end of the day.
I hope you know,
that there is no timeline for easing your way back into life.
Months will pass and you'll have no idea how
you made it through,
but you will.
And you know why you will?
Because your loved ones are right there,
right next to you,
catching every tear,
comforting you,
and doing everything they can,
in new ways,
just to get you through,
to the end of the days.
So, I hope you found comfort in reading these poems,
knowing your loved one is near.

One final poem,
from me to you Daddy.

Once hand in hand,
my father and I,
shared laughter and love beneath the Grecian skies,
where the Aegean sighs,
and memories lie.
His laughter echoed in the warm sea breeze,
a melody now lost among the olive trees.
Together we roamed,
carefree and wild,
in this land where I was a child.

Now, as I walk these familiar sands,
I feel his guiding hands.
The waves crash softly, a gentle refrain,
echoing the love now mingled with pain.
The mountains rise,
silent and strong,
witnesses to a grief that feels ever so wrong.
The depth of loss that I now face,
in this land where he once held a place,
I find a space,
to remember his smile,
and his loving grace.

When the sky meets the sea,
I search for traces of his spirit within me.
The deep blue seas hold my silent tears,
as I mourn the loss across the years.
Yet, in Greece's heart,
I find solace,
a sense of home.
Though grief is heavy,
the love remains,
in every wave and soft rain.
By the Aegean I feel him near,
gently whispering, "I am here".

Made in United States
North Haven, CT
11 November 2024